Macbeth
The Hidden Astrological Keys

GW00778035

Great works of literature are like stars;
they stay put, even as we draw them
into new constellations.

—Adam Kirsch

Macbeth

The Hidden Astrological Keys

PRISCILLA COSTELLO, M.A.

ADAPTED FROM

Shakespeare and the Stars

*The Hidden Astrological Keys to
Understanding the World's
Greatest Playwright*

IBIS PRESS
Lake Worth, FL

Published in 2018 by Ibis Press
A division of Nicolas-Hays, Inc.
P. O. Box 540206
Lake Worth, FL 33454-0206
www.ibispress.net

Distributed to the trade by
Red Wheel/Weiser, LLC
65 Parker St. • Ste. 7
Newburyport, MA 01950
www.redwheelweiser.com

ISBN 978-0-89254-177-5
Ebook: ISBN 978-0-89254-646-6

Library of Congress Cataloging-in-Publication Data
Available upon request

Book design and production by STUDIO 31
www.studio31.com

Cover painting: the Cobbe portrait, ca. 1610
Smile retouch by Mimi Alonzo
Photo of Mars by NASA
Cover design by STUDIO 31

Printed in the United States of America
[MG]

GENERAL INTRODUCTION: DID SHAKESPEARE REALLY USE ASTROLOGICAL SYMBOLS?

"It is the *stars*,/ The *stars* above us,
govern our conditions…" (*King Lear*)

"Methinks it should be now a huge
eclipse/ Of *sun* and *moon*…" (*Othello*)

"I know thy *constellation* is right apt
for this affair." (*Twelfth Night*)

Shakespeare's works are filled with references like these to heavenly bodies and stellar events. This isn't surprising since people of his time were more aware of the skies and the stars than we are: with no electric lights and few clocks, farmers, mariners, and the average Elizabethan looked to the sky to determine time and weather. Since personalities were classified in relation to specific planets (an early form of psychology) and medical practice was based on planetary types (or "temperaments"), the meanings of the astrological symbols were familiar to them.

For the illiterate (the majority) oral traditions passed down for generations made the astrological language familiar. The literate read yearly almanacs in English listing astrological omens. Educated Elizabethans grasped astrology's more profound implications since astrological language appeared frequently in religious writings. Steeped in the classical literature of ancient Greece and Rome, they knew that astrology is an integral part of an elegant, sophisticated, and intelligently-thought-out spiritual philosophy whose language and symbolism had been transmitted through the centuries and were part of lively discussion well into the 17th century (and still are today).

Like the members of Shakespeare's audience, his characters are also familiar with astrology.

> His dramatis personae speak of stars, planets, comets, meteors, eclipses, planetary aspects, predominance, conjunction, opposition, retrogradation, and all sorts of astro-meteorology. They know that the Dragon's Tail exerts an evil influence, that Mercury governs lying and thievery, that Luna [the Moon] rules vagabonds and idle fellows, that Saturn is malignant and Jupiter benevolent, that the signs of the zodiac rule the limbs and organs of the body, that planets influence cities and nations . . . Although they do not go into details regarding the technical workings of the science, his characters on the whole seem to possess a general knowledge of stellar influence on human destiny. —Johnstone Parr[1]

---

1 Johnstone Parr, *Tamburlaine's Malady and Other Essays on Astrology in Elizabethan Drama*, U. of Alabama Press, 1953, p. 64.

We don't catch many of the astrological allusions in Shakespeare's plays and understand their significance because we're no longer steeped in the grand worldview that was fundamental to Elizabethan thinking. We're conditioned in our time by the dominant beliefs of conventional materialistic science: that only physical things are real and that the only way to acquire knowledge is through five-sense perception. But for hundreds of years before Shakespeare's time the dominant paradigm was of a universe unfolding from Divinity in an orderly progression of hierarchical levels, down through the realm of the fixed stars, through the "crystalline spheres" of the seven classical planets, and ultimately into the physical world of human beings, animals, plants, and minerals. The fact that the planets are an integral part of this worldview justifies looking at Shakespeare's plays through the lens of astrology.

Each level is linked with all the levels above and below it, so that references to the planets trigger a host of associations on all the other levels. In a worldview in which the heavens are reflected on Earth and the realm of Earth mirrors the heavens, it is natural to see a connection between the glorious Sun that dominates the skies and the King who is the focus of court and country. Shimmering moonlight is symbolically reflected in the sheen of silver. Because this worldview allows for sympathetic resonances between all levels of creation, Shakespeare can write of tempests both external to King Lear and within his mind, of eclipses that portend the fall of kings, and of horses that eat each other when Macbeth murders King Duncan. Events on one level of being can reflect events on another.

Since Shakespeare's works reflect this generally accepted worldview, the vast majority of his characters' statements are overwhelmingly in line with the Renaissance astrological worldview familiar to his audience. Shakespeare naturally draws on familiar astrological symbolism as creative inspiration for his art, in both obvious and subtle ways. He uses it for various purposes: to establish time and its passage; to create characters in line with planetary associations; and to allude to themes and philosophical ideas embedded in these symbols. Most of his plays focus on one particular sign of the zodiac and its associated ruling planet with the "key" of the piece being conveyed by the language and allusions in the first (or second) scene.

The following discussion of this particular play (books by the same author about other Shakespearean plays are also available) begins with a summary of the story, and then reveals the play's key: the zodiacal sign and its associated planet. The main part uncovers the connections between aspects of the play and relevant astrological symbols, considering their significance from different perspectives and on different levels. Important key words are CAPITALIZED to make it easy for readers to identify core ideas associated with the sign and planet.

Since the worldview of Shakespeare's time is so comprehensive, his allusions are wide-ranging, encompassing the heavenly spheres, the human world on all its levels, and the world of nature. My explorations are equally wide-ranging: they include the mythological, the psychological, the philosophical, the religious or spiritual, the esoteric, and of course the mundane (references to gems and minerals, plants and animals, weather conditions, and even separate parts of the human body that were all correlated with the heavens).

I hope that the resulting wide-ranging discussion will intrigue perceptive play-goers and eager readers of Shakespeare's works who wish to explore their hidden depths from a new and different perspective, one that provides fresh insights into Shakespeare's extraordinary creations. His "capacious" consciousness, combined with literary craft, midwived a unique body of work that could only have been produced at that particular time by an individual having an unusual combination of literary artistry, astute perception, and vivid imagination, along with a profound understanding of philosophical, esoteric, and spiritual wisdom—which includes astrology. It is this combination of gifts and talents that has made his works vital and intriguing for over four centuries.

And now on to ... *MACBETH*.

(The ideas here are condensed from the chapter entitled "The Hidden Astrological Key to *Macbeth*" in *Shakespeare and the Stars: the Hidden Astrological Keys to Understanding the World's Greatest Playwright* published by Ibis Press in 2016.)

MACBETH
SCORPIO AND ITS RULER MARS

Even the evil meet with good fortune as long as their evil has
yet to mature. But when it's matured, that's when they meet
with evil. Even the good meet with bad fortune as long as
their good has yet to mature. But when it's matured,
that's when they meet with good fortune.

—-Dhammapada 9, translated by Thanissaro Bhikkhu

O, full of *scorpions* is my mind, dear wife!
—Macbeth (III, ii, 37)

THE STORY

In thunder and lightning, three witches meet on a heath
and plan an encounter with Macbeth. In the mean-
time, King Duncan of Scotland receives reports from a
wounded sergeant, a "bloody man", describing how the
acclaimed warrior Macbeth, along with his fellow gen-
eral Banquo, has put down an internal rebellion led by
the traitorous thane of Cawdor and has heroically mas-
sacred external invaders from Norway. Duncan declares
that he will transfer Cawdor's title to Macbeth. The three
"weird sisters" do appear suddenly to Macbeth and Banquo as they return from battle and predict that Macbeth,
now thane of Glamis, will become thane of Cawdor,
and eventually King. When Banquo asks the witches to
"look into the seeds of time" for him, he's told that he

will beget a line of kings though he will be none. Fuelled by the witches' prophecies, Macbeth's imagination as well as his fear is stirred and his ambition grows—especially when Duncan suddenly names his son Malcolm as his successor.

When the King arrives at Macbeth's castle, Macbeth is tempted by his presence and goaded by his wife to assassinate him in order to take the throne. After struggling with his conscience, Macbeth tells his wife he wants to cancel their plan. But Lady Macbeth needles her husband into proceeding with the plan to murder Duncan, who's drugged by her and stabbed by Macbeth that very night. Once he's killed Duncan, though, Macbeth's mind is disturbed and he regrets his deed. He forgets to leave the bloody weapons at the murder scene, and Lady Macbeth must return to the chamber to plant the gory daggers on Duncan's drugged grooms.

Macduff and Lennox arrive, pounding on the door to awaken a drunken porter, and discover the king's bloodied body. To prevent them from protesting their innocence, Macbeth kills the grooms. Anxious and suspicious, Duncan's sons flee to England and Ireland.

Once invested as King, Macbeth's conscience begins to trouble him even more. Beset by terrible dreams, his fear and insecurity lead him to arrange the killing of his former friend Banquo, who's begun to suspect that Macbeth murdered Duncan. Banquo's ghost appears to disrupt a royal banquet and disturb Macbeth who's also fearful and doubtful because Banquo's son Fleance escaped the hired murderers. Macbeth now actively seeks out the three witches, who promise that he cannot be destroyed until "Birnam wood come to Dunsinane" castle and that he's invincible unless he confronts someone "not of woman born." Reassured, Macbeth proceeds to order the massacre of the family of Macduff, around whom opposition to his rule has begun to coalesce. Scotland is suffering under the tyrant's rule.

Macduff himself has fled to England, where he seeks out Malcolm whose virtues are contrasted with Macbeth's vices. They and the English forces who have gathered there proceed to invade Scotland. Just before the final battle Lady Macbeth, now guilt-ridden, haunted, and sleepwalking at nights, commits suicide. A messenger reports that Birnam wood moves toward the castle and Macbeth realizes he's been manipulated by "juggling fiends." Disheartened but driven to fight, Macbeth arms and leaves the castle. In a final bloody encounter Macduff reveals that he had a caesarian birth (and thus is not "of woman born"), clashes with the "hell-hound" Macbeth, and beheads him. Duncan's son Malcolm is hailed as king, honors his fellow fighters as newly created "earls", and, promising to "perform in measure, time, and place" whatever else is needful, restores order.

The Key to Macbeth: Mars

Clues to the archetypal symbolism underlying *Macbeth* are dramatically revealed in both the first and second scenes of the play. Scene 1 is unusually brief—only 12 lines—and features three supernatural creatures: the malevolent witches who speak in ambiguities (the battle will be "lost and won") and invoke a clouded and contaminated atmosphere ("fog and filthy air"). We are in the realm of the occult. (More on that later.)

Scene ii, however, takes us into the human world, where battles are raging. An alarum sounds, characteristically the noise of war, and the first spoken words are "What bloody man is that?" A Captain reporting to King Duncan paints a picture of the tireless Macbeth's superhuman achievement in slaughtering the rebel leader Macdonwald:

> . . . brave Macbeth—well he deserves that
> name!—
> Disdaining Fortune, with his brandished
> steel
> Which smoked with bloody execution,
> Like Valour's minion
> Carved out his passage till he faced the slave,
> Which ne'er shook hands nor bade farewell
> to him,
> Till he unseamed him from the nave to
> th'chops,
> And fixed his head upon our battlements.
>
> (I, ii, 16-23)

Without the courtesies of Venus (like a gentlemanly shaking of hands), Macbeth confronts the head of the rebel forces, the "merciless Macdonwald", and in hand-to-hand combat slices him from nave (navel) to the chops (jaw). King Duncan, upon hearing the Captain's vivid description of the battle, exclaims, 'O valiant cousin! Worthy gentleman!" (I, ii, 24) This aggression is celebrated as a defense of the state and of established authority, and so our first impression of the generals is supremely positive.

To reinforce our immediate impression of Macbeth as an undaunted warrior, Shakespeare doubles the battle: not only must Macbeth defeat rebellious forces that threaten the state from within, but he must also take arms against the opportunistic Norwegians who seize the chance to invade from without. The Captain assures the King that neither Macbeth nor Banquo were disheartened by this second threat: ". . . I must report they were/ As cannons overcharged with double cracks/ So they doubly redoubled strokes upon the foe." (I, i, 36-8) The word "double" will assume a more sinister meaning later when the witches begin their incantation around the cauldron with "Double, double, toil and trouble", recalling this unusual double combat as well as the "double dealing" that is rampant throughout the play.

Many key words in this scene—"bloody", "revolt", "soldier", "brave", "merciless", "valour", "quarrel", "execution", "conflict"—point inexorably to MARS, the god of WAR. Mars, dubbed "the red planet", has specific rulership over blood. We are unquestionably in the arena of Mars.

Like all astrological symbols, Mars is double-sided, as is illustrated by two quite different classical interpretations. The Greeks' name for their god of war was Ares. They considered him unevolved, a symbol of unthinking brute and blundering force with a low level of conscious development and little self-awareness.

By contrast, the Romans exalted Mars as defender of the state, appropriate for an empire that depended on military might for its expansion and consolidation. At the beginning of the play, when he's earned praise and honor as captain of the King's forces, Macbeth is almost the literal incarnation of this more positive Roman Mars. To defend the state, under the direction of a legitimate king, is highly esteemed. Duncan judges that the captain's words and wounds "smack of honour both." This honor applies to Macbeth as well, who has dominated the field. Ross even dubs him "Bellona's bridegroom," an extremely important mythological allusion for it depicts Macbeth as actually married to the Roman goddess of war. He's at one with her bellicose spirit, and exhibits all the positive qualities of the Roman Mars. (I, ii, 54)

In astrological tradition prior to the modern era, though, Mars had a poor reputation as the "lesser malefic"—not bringing as many difficulties as Saturn, the "greater malefic", but coinciding with bad luck or ill fortune nonetheless. Consistent with the more reprehensible side of Mars, as the story progresses Macbeth devolves into a "bloody-sceptered" tyrant instead of legitimate ruler, a murderer of defenseless women and children instead of a hero in battle against armed men, and finally a "dead butcher" mated with a "fiend-like queen." (V, xi, 35) Ironically, just as at the beginning he decapitated the traitorous Macdonwald and mounted his head on the Scottish battlements, at the end *he* is decapitated and *his* head is displayed as a trophy of war. Symbolically, since Macbeth has progressively become more obsessed and less rational, he has "lost his head." (It's also significant that the head is the part of the body ruled by Mars!)

In keeping with the spirit of Mars (who is too impatient to allow for lulls in the action), *Macbeth* is the shortest of Shakespeare's plays, and the action proceeds directly and precipitously (like the Martian arrow loosed from a bow) once it begins. The pace of the play is relentless, and Macbeth acts in accord with it. After his second encounter with the weird sisters, he vows, "From this moment/ The very firstlings of my heart shall be/ The firstlings of my hand. And even now,/ To crown my thoughts with acts, be it thought and done." (IV, i, 162-5) Without reflection or hesitation, his intentions will immediately manifest in Mars-like action.

The Zodiacal Sign of Scorpio, Ruled by Mars

Mars is traditionally assigned rulership of Scorpio, the eighth sign of the zodiac. As a tragedy and for dramatic purposes, the play concerns itself with the uglier and more repugnant expressions of the sign Scorpio along with the downsides of its ruler Mars.

Scorpio is probably the most complex and difficult zodiacal symbol to unspool, encompassing profound areas of challenge, mystery, and taboo: the secrets of birth, the fearsomeness of death, and the enigma of an afterlife; the compelling power of sexual desire with all its ecstasies and degradations; the forbidden realm of the occult, both exalting and damning (and damned); the challenge of wielding power in the sphere of politics; and the use of depth psychology to probe the inner psyche.

Individuals with strong Scorpio energy in their horoscopes may attain positions of influence without being elected, like Mahatma Gandhi who influenced millions and altered history or Bill Gates who made millions and midwived the transition into the computer age. Other Sun in Scorpio figures like Teddy Roosevelt, Charles de Gaulle, and Hillary Clinton have participated dramatically in the political process through conducting conventional campaigns and occupying established offices. Politics and leadership positions offer particular challenges for Scorpios; you may run for office with the most idealistic of motives—to serve the people who elect you and legislate for the good of the state—but all too easily become bogged down in the quagmires of the political process, tempted by money and influence and lured into egotistic displays of bombastic rhetoric.

Because Scorpios often exude a charged energy through a forceful personality as a result of sustained focus, a developed will power, and consistent self-discipline, others often fear them or are in awe of them. It's easy to impute sinister motives to a Scorpio even when the Scorpio person may be working to bring about the greatest good for the greatest number. Whether a force for good or ill, the Scorpio type is magnetically compelling. The challenges for a Scorpio are daunting: coping with physical desires; finding a creative outlet for intense feelings; keeping psychologically healthy; and exerting appropriate influence in a chosen sphere. All of these themes are explored in *Macbeth*.

The Scorpio type is especially driven by strong and passionate DESIRES, usually manifested as a hunger for power, sexual pleasure, or wealth (or all of these). Gaining the fruits of these desires is not necessarily evil, unless you use illegal or immoral means to do so. The first step to a healthy integration of these desires into your life is to acknowledge your lust for power, or the intensity of your sexual drive, or your yearning for money. If you feel GUILT about any of these, the tendency is to SUPPRESS DESIRE, which leads to various personality kinks, perversions, and displacements that can cause you to act out in destructive ways—destructive to yourself and possibly to others around you. GUILT can also trigger an overactive CONSCIENCE, so that regret for past actions haunts you while desires still persist.

For Macbeth, what drives him is the desire for POWER, his AMBITION to be king of Scotland. This is confirmed by both Lady Macbeth who describes her husband as "not without ambition" (I, v, 17) and Macbeth himself who admits that the only spur to his intent is "vaulting ambition"—but adds ominously that it "o'erleaps itself/ And falls on th'other—" (I, vii, 25-8). Then begins the terrible struggle within Macbeth between acting on this desire or restraining it.

The struggle is made more complex by the influence of the three witches, who predict his elevation to kingship, and by the persuasion of his wife, who urges him on to greatness by "catching the nearest way." We know he's tormented by their combined influence and by his own lust for power which conflicts with social and cultural inhibitions because he laments, "O, full of scorpions is my mind, dear wife!" (III, ii, 37) The SCORPION, of course, is the creature associated with the sign Scorpio, and the pictograph for the sign includes an upturned stinger that warns of danger and threatens death.

Another animal associated with the sign Scorpio is the SNAKE, a powerful symbol in the West. In the story of Adam and Eve in the Garden of Eden the snake represents the first couple's desire for knowledge and consequently is a personification of temptation and evil. There are many telling references to snakes in *Macbeth*, especially Lady Macbeth's advice to her husband: "To beguile the time,/ Look like the time; bear welcome in your eye,/ Your hand, your tongue; look like the innocent flower,/ But be the *serpent* under 't." (I, v, 61-4)

Other animals associated with the dark side of Scorpio are black birds such as ravens and all creatures of the night such as owls. Owls are mentioned several times during the play, most significantly immediately before Duncan's murder when Lady Macbeth hears it shrieking, and then after the murder when an owl achieves ascendency by killing a noble falcon. Falcons fly at higher altitudes than owls, implying that the higher has been brought down by the lower.

Before the banquet and just after Macbeth has enlisted hired assassins to kill Banquo and his son, Macbeth again invokes darkness to hide his deeds and refers to a black bird: "Light thickens, and the *crow*/ Makes wing to the rooky wood;/ Good things of day begin to droop and drowse,/ Whiles night's *black* agents to their preys do rouse." (III, ii, 51-4) As always in Shakespeare's works, dominant images such as these reinforce other clues to the archetypal zodiacal sign to which the play is keyed.

Not just black birds, but all things of the color BLACK are associated with the sign Scorpio, often decorated with splashes of RED. Innumerable references to black night and to blood stud the play from beginning to end. These are the main colors mentioned throughout.

The Water Element and Emotions: Control versus Repression

Scorpio is a WATER sign, the second of three in the zodiacal pantheon. Shakespeare inserts many and significant references to water in the play, like Lady Macbeth's confident assumption that a small amount can wash away their sin: "A little water clears us of this deed" (II, ii, 65). Even more stunning is Macbeth's lament after the murder of King Duncan; not only will "a little water" not wash away his crime, but he questions whether "all great Neptune's ocean [can] wash this blood/ Clean from my hand? No, this my hand will rather/ The multitudinous seas incarnadine,/ Making the green one red." (II, ii, 58-61) The power attributed to water, of purification, has been reversed, and Macbeth's dreadful deed corrupts the entire ocean. After Macbeth has added the death of Banquo to his account, Macbeth says, "I am in blood/Stepped in so far that, should I wade no more,/ Returning were as tedious as go o'er." (III, iv, 135-7) His previous comment foreshadows a complete transformation of the sea; it no longer consists of water but is now entirely blood, as if Macbeth's blood-letting has flooded the world.

Water symbolizes the emotional level of each human being, and individuals with many water signatures in their horoscopes are motivated primarily by feelings. One of the key challenges for the Scorpio type is dealing with emotions. The archetypal Scorpio is sensitive to emotional undercurrents and may experience more intense and more deeply felt EMOTIONS than most, which they attempt to CONTROL. Because intense feelings can be overwhelming and not easily integrated, the Scorpio person may opt for EMOTIONAL REPRESSION. This correlates perfectly with the specific manifestation of water associated with Scorpio, its frozen form as ice. The typically repressed Scorpio can become fixated on emotional issues that may either fester openly or be driven below conscious awareness. Buried in the unconscious, these emotional complexes can drive actions compulsively and uncontrollably.

Scorpio types seem fated to deal with the most negative emotions, such as jealousy, envy, resentment, bitterness, hatred, vengefulness, and anger, even escalating to rage—the stuff of soap operas, grand operas, and the best-remembered tragedies. These may also include FEAR and, in the extreme, even paranoia and terror. Of all of these, fear is the emotion that most colors the atmosphere of *Macbeth*. Scorpios in particular have the task of transmuting these negative emotions into kindness, compassion, and unselfish love—a very difficult task.

It's emotionally exhausting to keep strong emotions at bay or to keep them below the conscious threshold. One consequence is that you can lose the capacity to feel anything, even the more desirable and normally accessible emotions.

We see the intensity of Macbeth's emotions from the beginning of the play, when he reacts sensitively and strongly to the witches' declarations by being startled, fearful, and shaken. But by the end of the drama, Macbeth is so out of touch emotionally that he has entirely lost the capacity to respond. When women cry within, mourning the Queen, he who trembled to think of murdering Duncan cannot feel any alarm or disquiet:

I have almost forgot the taste of *fears*.
The time has been, my senses would have
    cooled
To hear a night-shriek, and my fell of hair
Would at a dismal treatise rouse and stir
As life were in't. I have supped full with
    horrors.
Direness, familiar to my slaughterous
    thoughts,
Cannot once start me.

                          (V, v, 9-15)

Macbeth is so emotionally dead that when he is told the reason for the women crying, that the Queen is dead, he can only remark, "She should have died hereafter . . . " (V, v, 17) Then comes the most powerful statement of emotional numbness in all of Western literature:

To-morrow, and to-morrow, and to-morrow
Creeps in this petty pace from day to day
To the last syllable of recorded time,
And all our yesterdays have lighted fools
The way to dusty death. Out, out, brief
    candle.
Life's but a walking shadow, a poor player
That struts and frets his hour upon the stage,
And then is heard no more. It is a tale
Told by an idiot, full of sound and fury,
Signifying nothing.

                        (V, v, 18-27)

As a deliberate contrast to Macbeth's managing of his emotions (or mismanagement since they're ultimately suppressed), Shakespeare presents Macduff as a foil. Macduff is told shockingly and unexpectedly that his castle was surprised and his wife and children savagely slaughtered. You can't imagine more horrible news for a husband and father. But Shakespeare has Macduff respond in ways that outline deliberate strategies to cope with powerful feelings triggered by traumatic events. At this terrible emotional blow, at first Macduff cannot even speak. When he tries to, encouraged by Malcolm, his first attempts are in choppy lines as he reels at the enormity of his loss.

> MALCOLM: What, man, ne'er pull your hat upon
>   your brows.
>   Give sorrow words. The grief that does not
>   speak
>   Whispers the o'erfraught heart and bids it
>   break.
> MACDUFF: My children too?
> ROSS: Wife, children, servants, all
>   That could be found.
> MACDUFF: And I must be from thence!
>   My wife killed too? . . .
>   He has no children. All my pretty ones?
>   Did you say all? O hell-kite! All?
>   What, all my pretty chickens and their dam
>   At one fell swoop?
>   (IV, iii, 209-14, 217-20)

When Malcolm urges Macduff to "Dispute it like a man", Macduff delivers this extremely important statement: "I shall do so./ But I must also feel it as a man." Macduff acknowledges the necessity of staying with his feelings, however uncomfortable, and not banishing them from conscious awareness: "I cannot but remember such things were/ That were most precious to me." (IV, iii, 221-5) In this brief exchange, we can perceive four stages of handling grief that Shakespeare sequences: initial silence, groping speech, acknowledged deep feeling, and consciously sustained remembrance.

In line with the more positive Mars, Macduff is urged to go one step farther: to convert the emotional energy of the grief he feels at the slaughter of his family into sharp and focused REVENGE on the perpetrator. Macduff thus becomes the legitimate executioner of Macbeth, because he has just cause, a personal motive. Eliminating Macbeth satisfies an impersonal goal too: to exorcize the evil that has infected the country and restore the body politic to health.

Scorpio and the Will

Managing emotions introduces yet another key issue for Scorpio, that of the WILL and WILL POWER. What does it mean to have a strong will? What is will "power" exactly? We associate it first with the internal ability to control our feelings, desires and actions, refraining from destructive ones (like risking our resources in gambling or undermining our health by overeating) and opting for ones that improve our physical or mental health (like exercise) or benefit us spiritually (like prayer).

From ancient times and into the Elizabethan period, the will was thought of as uniquely positioned to consider the evidence of the senses, memories of past occurrences, and accumulated knowledge and understanding, and then to decide on the most rational action to take. Both esoteric philosophy and the Christian religion acknowledge that human beings have free will; each assumes that the best use of the will is to choose what is "good." Both religious doctrine and spiritual practice stress the need for using the will to control the appetites—sometimes literally, demanding both fasting and chastity. The challenge is, as it has always been, not to allow imposed control to become excessive, thereby turning our zeal for improvement into an obsessive, almost fanatical self-deprivation.

Another way of exerting the will is to externalize it, using it to influence or control others' behavior to make them do what you want them to do (thereby undermining their own will and integrity). Methods used to subvert another's better intentions may include appeals to baser instincts (like lust, greed, or selfishness) or blatant manipulation using various persuasive techniques.

One of the influences driving Macbeth to his doomed end is his wife. She uses *her* will power to urge her husband along the criminal path to achieving his desire. She ultimately takes CONTROL of the situation herself, advising him to "put/ This night's great business into my dispatch." (I, v, 65-6) It is she who devises the plan to drug Duncan's grooms and to leave bloody daggers next to their sleeping bodies so that they'll appear to be guilty of the murder. Confidently, she directs him to "Leave all the rest to me." (I, v, 71) Macbeth has entertained doubts about killing Duncan, fearing that others will use similar methods on him: "... we but teach/ Bloody instructions, which, being taught, return/ To plague th'inventor. This even-handed justice/ Commends th'ingredients of our poisoned chalice/ To our own lips." (I, vii, 8-12) (This is an insightful comment about the workings of karma.) He's also aware that he is Duncan's kinsman, subject, and host, all strong grounds for sparing the King, who is portrayed as a virtuous and capable leader. Macbeth admits that his essential motivation is at root nothing but "vaulting ambition." His wife knows this too, and she becomes a powerful influence directing him to murder the rightful King.

Mars, Masculinity, and the Roots of Violence: Lady Macbeth's Manipulative Technique

Just as Venus is the pre-eminent symbol of the feminine, Mars is the outstanding symbol of the masculine. Yet Scorpio, like all the water signs, is considered yin or feminine. It's especially challenging for men born with the Sun or a number of other planets in the sign Scorpio to acknowledge their feminine sides; many over-compensate by becoming bossy and bullying or even villainous and criminal. They may become terrified of their inner sensitivity and vulnerability, which they interpret as weakness.

As a Scorpio type, Macbeth is especially sensitive to challenges to his masculinity. So when Macbeth tells his wife that he'll go no further with their plans to murder Duncan, she knows just how to get him back on board. As he hesitates, Lady Macbeth needles him by questioning his maleness:

> Art thou *afeard*
> To be the same in thine own act and valour
> As thou art in desire? Wouldst thou have
>   that
> Which thou esteem'st the ornament of life,
> And live a *coward* in thine own esteem . . . ?
>   (I, vii, 39-43)

Macbeth is well aware of her tactic, and protests, "Prithee, peace./ I dare do all that may become a man;/ Who dares do more is none." (I, vii, 45-7) Relentless in pressing the point, Lady Macbeth acidly continues: "What beast was't, then/ That made you break this enterprise to me?/ When you durst do it, then you were a man . . . " (I, vii, 47-9) In answer to his feebly expressed fear of failure, she presses him (with an implied sexual taunt) to "screw your courage to the sticking-place,/ And we'll not fail." (I, vii, 60-1) She literally shames him into killing the King.

Lady Macbeth thus provokes painful feelings in Macbeth of fearing dishonor or disgrace. What greater humiliation can there be for the heroic Macbeth described in the opening scene of the play than to be accused of being effeminate? Lady Macbeth chastises her husband again immediately following the murder, when Macbeth hears a voice cry out that he's murdered sleep and he refuses to return to the king's chamber with the bloody daggers, saying, "I'll go no more./ I *am afraid* to think what I have done,/ Look on't again I dare not." (II, ii, 48-50) Lady Macbeth herself must place the weapons by the sleeping grooms. On her return she reproaches Macbeth with "My hands are of your colour, but I *shame*/ To wear a heart so white." (II, ii, 62-3) Taking charge, it is she who gives him instructions: to retire to their chamber, to put on his nightgown, and not to be lost in regretful thoughts.

Understanding her husband's character, Lady Macbeth employs the same strategy later when Macbeth disrupts the banquet held to consolidate his position with the Scottish lords. Upon seeing the gory locks of the murdered Banquo's ghost, Macbeth appears to be having a fit, and blurts out strange phrases that upset the guests. Attempting to jolt the distraught Macbeth into an awareness of the social occasion, she challenges him with "Are you a *man*?" Macbeth protests, but once the Ghost vanishes, Lady Macbeth taunts him again: "What, quite *unmann'd* in folly?" (III, iv, 72)

Macbeth has learned Lady Macbeth's strategy of attacking a man's masculinity for he uses it himself with the assassins he's hired to kill Banquo and his son. In a previous meeting, he's already planted the seed-idea in the hired killers that Banquo is to blame for their misfortunes. Now he challenges them to do something about it: "Do you find/ Your patience so predominant in your nature/ That you can let this go?" To which the murderers protest, "We are *men*, my liege." (III, i, 87-9, 93) Macbeth proceeds to insult them by calling them dogs. Fueled by Scorpionic emotions of both anger and resentment, they then agree to murder the two. Just as Lady Macbeth manipulated Macbeth into murdering Duncan, so Macbeth manipulates the two murderers into killing Banquo and his son. Like Lady Macbeth, too, he has a well-thought-out plan to ensure the crime's success.

Uncannily, Shakespeare has the psychological source of violence, as we now understand it, absolutely right. Contemporary psychology offers some cogent insights into Macbeth's behavior that are in accord with Shakespeare's depiction. In a series of books and articles exploring the roots of violence, psychiatrist Dr. James Gilligan concludes, after many years of experience with prisoners and those in prison mental wards, that "the basic psychological motive, or cause, of violent behavior is the wish to ward off or eliminate the feeling of shame and humiliation, a feeling that is painful and can even be intolerable and overwhelming, and replace it with its opposite, the feeling of pride."[2]

---

2 James Gilligan, *Violence: Our Deadly Epidemic and Its Causes*, New York: Putnam's, 1996, pp. 231.

Why, after being so acclaimed on the battlefield and awarded with land and titles, would Macbeth be vulnerable to shame and humiliation? One reason is that opportunities for glory on the battlefield have passed; he's back in civilian territory. His fixation on becoming king is perhaps a substitute for battlefield glory. It would be a logical step up the ladder, another way to exhibit his power and potency. Macbeth, though, is not a trained or experienced political leader—he's a warrior. This illustrates the danger in attempting to fulfill a role for which you have no experience or talent but only ego motives.

Another reason is King Duncan's abrupt and curiously-timed announcement, immediately following Macbeth's great achievement, that the kingdom will pass to his eldest son Malcolm. At that time rulership of Scotland was established through election by the nobles. It wasn't hereditary. Surely as the most important of Duncan's supporters and defenders, Macbeth would be the logical choice to take the reins of the kingdom. Perhaps this is precisely why Duncan chooses this moment to decree that the next in line will be his own progeny. Macbeth instantly recognizes this as an obstacle—and an insult. He's been publicly slighted. Lady Macbeth's castigations fall onto a newly-sensitized psyche.

The Witches' Persuasive Technique: Equivocation

Lady Macbeth's Scorpionic manipulative technique is that of humiliation, shaming Macbeth by questioning his masculinity in order to override his will. The witches are as adept in Scorpionic-style manipulation as Lady Macbeth, only they use a different strategy. The principal persuasive technique they practice on Macbeth is "equivocation": the use of ambiguous language with intent to mislead or deceive.

To make Macbeth more confident about the truth of their prophecies, the first three pronouncements they deliver are simple statements that are true or do come true. Macbeth *is* Thane of Glamis. Within minutes of their pronouncement that he'll be Thane of Cawdor, Ross arrives to tell Macbeth that Duncan has bestowed this new title on him. So it's logical for him to think that he'll become King. And he does become King—though a question nags at us: Would this have happened had he not taken criminal action to bring it about? Or do the witches suggest it because they know that impatient ambition will drive him to take immoral steps to *make* it happen?

But the second set of three prophecies, dramatized when Macbeth actively seeks the witches, is delivered partly in statements and partly in riddles, and by apparitions and not the witches themselves. The warning to beware Macduff seems reasonable and resonates with Macbeth's own fear of him. But then he's told to "Be bloody, bold, and resolute. Laugh to scorn/ The power of man, for *none of woman born/* Shall harm Macbeth." (IV, i, 95-7) He interprets this to mean that he's invincible, but he's disabused of this when Macduff, sword in hand, challenges him to hand-to-hand combat after Macbeth's castle is breached, and reveals that he "was from his mother's womb/ Untimely ripped." (V, x, 15-6) Since his birth was caesarean, Macduff is technically not "of woman born." The witches told the precise truth but in such a way as to mislead Macbeth into thinking that he's unkillable.

The third phantom delivers what would seem to be the most improbable possibility: "Macbeth shall never vanquished be until/ Great Birnam Wood to high Dunsinane Hill/ Shall come against him." (IV, i, 106-10) Confidently, Macbeth responds "That will never be./ Who can impress the forest, bid the tree/ Unfix his earthbound root? Sweet bodements, good!" (IV, I, 110-12) So seductive are these assurances that Macbeth mistakes the evil intent behind the prophecies for "good."

Both the second and third pronouncements encourage him to be arrogant, to scorn the threat of the invading English and Scottish forces, and to continue to trust in the witches' words:

> Bring me no more reports. Let them fly all.
> Till Birnam Wood remove to Dunsinane
> I cannot taint with fear. What's the boy
>   Malcolm?
> Was he not born of woman? The spirits that
>   know
> All mortal conseqences have pronounced me
>   thus:

'Fear not, Macbeth. No man that's born of
  woman
Shall e'er have power upon thee.'

(V, iii, 1-7)

Macbeth soon realizes the extent of the witches'
duplicity when a messenger reports that he sees the wood
begin to move, and Macbeth's determination weakens: "I
pall in resolution, and *begin/ To doubt th'equivocation of the
fiend,/ That lies like truth.*" The witches have subtly, both
at the beginning of the drama and near its end, influenced his catastrophic descent into deceit, murder, and
ultimately dishonor and despair through their leading
and misleading words.

This theme of equivocation is introduced earlier and
made explicit by the drunken Porter. Unsteady on his feet
as he staggers to open the castle gate immediately after
Duncan's murder, he delivers a long monologue studded
with instances of double-dealing: "Faith, here's an *equiv-
ocator*, that could swear in both the scales against either
scale, who committed treason enough for God's sake, yet
could not *equivocate* to heaven. O, come in, *equivocato*r."
(II, iii, 7-11) He seems to be describing Macbeth as well
as the witches.

The drunken porter introduces yet another associa-
tion with the sign Scorpio. Because of the potential for
emotional repression mentioned earlier, the Scorpionic
personality may suffer from various ADDICTIONS or COM-
PULSIONS. Among these is alcoholism. Duncan's guards

are vulnerable to Lady Macbeth's plan because they are drugged *and* made drunk and lie in "swinish sleep." Immediately following the murder, the porter ruminates about the effects of alcohol, especially on sexual performance (also a Scorpionic topic):

> Lechery, sir, it provokes, and unprovokes
> it provokes the desire but it takes away the
> performance. Therefore, much drink may
> be said to be an *equivocator* with lechery: it
> makes him and it mars him; it sets him on
> and it takes him off; it persuades him and
> disheartens him; makes him stand to and
> not stand to; in conclusion, *equivocates* him
> in a sleep, and, giving him the lie, leaves him.
>
> (II, iii, 26-33)

This eerily describes the witches' effect on Macbeth, from the beginning when he vacillates about killing Duncan through to the end when he at first determines to withstand a siege and then changes his mind, arming and leaving the castle.

Besides alcoholism, another instance of obsessive-compulsive behavior (associated with Scorpio) is Lady Macbeth's repeated washing of her hands in the sleepwalking scene just before she commits suicide. Her repetitive actions are observed covertly both by her gentlewoman and a doctor brought along as a witness.

DOCTOR: . . . Look, how she rubs her hands.

GENTLEWOMAN: It is an accustomed action
with her, to seem thus washing her
hands. I have known her continue in this
a quarter of an hour. . . .

LADY MACBETH: Out, damned spot; out, I
say. . . . What, will these hands ne'er be
clean? . . . Here's the smell of the blood
still. All the perfumes of Arabia will not
sweeten this little hand. O, O, O!

(V, i, 23-6, 30, 37, 42-3)

Scorpio and the Occult

The Scorpio individual is drawn to exploring realms that are hidden or suppressed, that are considered forbidden or dangerous, especially those that society considers taboo. So the sign Scorpio has to do with the OCCULT, and with invisible entities that might be either spontaneously experienced or deliberately contacted through a variety of established methods. Actually anything "occult" is merely that which is secret or hidden from view, the implication being that "occult" entities are not perceptible through the five senses.

Taking the realm of the occult seriously means that you're willing to explore the possible existence of invisible energies and entities. If so, long-established tradition recommends that you be prepared or initiated before encountering such entities from alternate and immaterial dimensions—or your physical, emotional, and mental health can suffer.

The sign Scorpio has particularly to do with pre-birth or after-death states, and so especially with mediumship and the ability to see ghosts of the departed (as Macbeth sees the dead Banquo). But the study of the occult embraces more than this. The occult tradition is

> . . . a coherent intellectual stream that has roots in metaphysics, cosmology and religion and which has tried to bring together widely disparate aspects of God's Creation within a complex structure of connections, sympathies and affinities. Within its realm are numerous sub-systems such as magic, astrology, demonology, Kabbalah, numerology, pyramidism, divination, theurgy and much else. An occult quality is one that is hidden from the senses, as opposed to a manifest quality that is readily apprehended. As such it would come to include the more supernatural elements of normative religion, such as providence, prophecy and millenarianism.[3]

Although a variety of unearthly beings appear in Shakespeare's plays (fairies in *A Midsummer Nights Dream*; Greek gods and goddesses in *Cymbeline* and *The Tempest*), *Macbeth* is the *only* play of Shakespeare's in which witches appear. This play is Shakespeare's dark-

---

3 David S. Katz, *The Occult Tradition: From the Renaissance to the Present Day*, London: Pimlico, 2007, pp. 1–2.

est depiction of the occult realm, focusing exclusively on the dark side and presenting only powers that toy with human beings for fell purposes, that gleefully instigate violent and evil acts, and that enjoy upsetting order by creating disorder. So successful is Shakespeare in creating a vortex of malevolent forces in this work that many actors have a superstitious fear of even speaking the play's name. They refer to it as 'That Play", or "The Scottish Play", or, in the case of a joking Peter O'Toole, "The Harry Lauder Show."

The atmosphere of evil generated by performances of the play may derive in part from characters in the play deliberately summoning dark forces. One of the established methods for actively contacting occult entities, whether good or evil, is INVOCATION: calling upon a power or various powers to aid one or to perform a certain act. Lady Macbeth becomes a witch-like figure, invoking clearly negative entities when she calls to them: "Come, you spirits that tend on mortal thoughts, unsex me here,/ And fill me from the crown to the toe top-full/ Of direst cruelty! . . . Come to my woman's breasts,/ And take my milk for gall, you murd'ring ministers. . . . Come, thick night,/And pall thee in the dunnest smoke of *hell.* . . ." (I, v, 38-41, 45-6, 48-9) This transforms her into one possessed by the dark entities she's summoned.

On several occasions Macbeth also appeals to the black powers. Soon after hearing of the prophecies and then witnessing Duncan's proclamation of his son as "Prince of Cumberland", next in line to the throne, he demands, "Stars, hide your fires,/ Let not light see my black and deep desires;/ The eye wink at the hand; yet let that be/ Which the eye fears, when it is done, to see." (I, iv, 50-3) Before Banquo's killing, he petitions, "Come, seeling night,/ Scarf up the tender eye of pitiful day,/ And with thy bloody and invisible hand/ Cancel and tear to pieces that great bond/ Which keeps me pale." (III, ii, 47-51) Literally calling on blackness and intentionally invoking the dark powers, Macbeth abrogates the "great bond"—his connection to a moral universe in which he is bound by various roles and responsibilities to his fellow human beings in accord with his place in the grand hierarchy.

Entities contacted by means such as invocation are not necessarily evil. Neither, probably, were the historical models for the "weird sisters": likely local wise women, perhaps the village herbalists, who might have had some intuitive ability. ("Wyrd" is a Celtic term for oracles inspired by visions and thus capable of prophecy.)

Over the centuries Christianity's unrelenting disapproval of pagan traditions, in which women prophetesses figured prominently, led to their demonization. This condemnation of females and their transformation into "witches" came about because of a combination of anti-paganism and anti-feminism. But it's true that the female entities that toy with Macbeth *are* clearly malevolent. This is implied from the opening of the play: they meet in awful weather, "thunder, lightning, or in rain"; the atmosphere around them is one of "fog and filthy air"; and they inhabit a morally questionable universe in which "Fair is foul, and foul is fair." (I, i, 1-11) By scene iii, when they meet on the heath, they have been "killing swine", and are plotting revenge on a sailor's wife by tormenting her husband at sea.

The witches do influence Macbeth to actively court the dark forces. The first terrible deed that Macbeth commits, the murder of a kinsman, guest, and king, catalyzes a burgeoning career in crime, one that inaugurates his slide into an inner hell. Shakespeare signals this within minutes of the murder of Duncan, for the porter unconsciously and ironically describes himself as the doorman of the doomed, saying "Here's a knocking indeed! If a man were porter of hell-gate, he should have [a grand] old [time] turning the key." (II, iii, 1-2) It hardly seems accidental that the servant who stays with Macbeth until the calamitous end is named "Seyton", which would probably be pronounced "Satan."

Issues for Scorpio: Temptation, Sin, and Evil

In the Medieval Age that preceded Shakespeare's era, western culture was obsessed with the idea that the forces of good and evil were at war with each other and that the battleground was the human soul. The battle was lost if you succumbed either to inner desires or to outer persuasion to do the forbidden. In either case it was a given that TEMPTATION was constantly present. To be "tempted" is to be enticed into doing something unwise or morally wrong. Issues of succumbing to or resisting desire, of indulging in or refraining from temptation (in all its various forms) have always traditionally been associated with the astrological sign Scorpio.

How do you know which actions are permissible and which are not? You look to established moral and ethical codes to help you differentiate between intentions, decisions, and actions that are "good" or "right" and those that are "bad" or "wrong." In the West you might look first at the Ten Commandments in the Bible's Old Testament, which are described as being written by the finger of God (Exodus 31:18) and thus divinely prescribed. To transgress these directives means that one has fallen into SIN: one has violated divine law. One of these commandments explicitly prohibits murder. Presumably exposure to such established and culturally-sanctioned moral codes, transmitted through parents, the extended family, the educational system, and religious institutions, helps you internalize principles that encourage you to love and to care for yourself and others.

Macbeth definitely knows the codes of his culture: he's expected to serve his sovereign, to honor his guest as a protective host, and to be loyal to a kinsman. He also hints at an awareness of greater consequences to his soul should he do what is proscribed—he fears that ending Duncan's life would imperil "the life to come." (I, vii, 7)

Acting in ways that will have destructive consequences for ourselves or others brings us back to the topic of the will and the strength of our will power. Along with the mental awareness of moral codes and influences, it's necessary to have strong character, with the ability to self-inhibit in order to resist temptation.

To dramatize the fact that people may be tempted but not necessarily succumb, Shakespeare provides Banquo as a foil to Macbeth. At the first appearance of the three witches, Banquo asks them to give prophecies to him as they have for his fellow thane, but qualifies it by saying, "Speak then to me, *who neither beg nor fear/ Your favours nor your hate.*" (I, iii, 58-9) He's careful to distance himself from them and their influence. When Macbeth solicits Banquo's support ("If you shall cleave to my consent when 'tis,/ It shall make honour for you." [ii, I, 24-5]), Banquo emphasizes his own integrity by saying "So I lose none/ In seeking to augment it, but still keep/ My bosom franchised and allegiance clear ..." (II, i, 26-7) This reveals an inner commitment to his own principles and a resistance to Macbeth's influence should it lead to a dishonorable action. Banquo opts for a consistency between his internal image of himself and his external behavior.

Banquo has another quality that enables him to resist temptation: the perceptive ability to discern the witches' true nature. When Ross arrives with the news that Macbeth is to be dubbed thane of Cawdor, Banquo speaks (in an aside), "What, can the *devil* speak true?" (I, iii, 105) Noticing that Macbeth is distracted by the witches' prophecies, he presciently warns Macbeth, ". . . 'tis strange,/ And oftentimes to win us to our harm/ The *instruments of darkness* tell us truths,/ Win us with honest trifles, to betray 's/ In deepest consequence." (I, iii, 120-4) Later he also intuits that Macbeth has acted criminally to achieve the throne: "Thou has it now: King, Cawdor, Glamis, all/ As the weird women promised; and I fear/ Thou played'st most foully for't." (III, i, 1-3)

How would the audience of Shakespeare's time account for the intrusion of the devil and its agents into the human world? The worldview of his time assumed that resonant bonds of sympathy linked different levels of creation to each other, so that higher levels could influence the lower. We still petition the help of God/ Goddess, or our "good" or guardian angel, or other helpful spirits. The Elizabethans also believed that the lower could affect the higher. The very lowest level of creation, sometimes thought to be EVIL because it's farthest from God, is personified as the devil or demons or other unnatural creatures like the "weird women." For many, both then and now, this realm and the entities thought to inhabit it are real—and actively malevolent. They tempt us by encouraging us to willfully violate moral principles: to harm ourselves, others, even the Earth itself, as they do.

But here's "the rub"—and the critical issues especially pertinent to the sign Scorpio. Who or what is most responsible for Macbeth's succumbing to the temptation to murder Duncan? The dark powers appearing in the play as the witches and possessing the person of Lady Macbeth? Circumstance? Macbeth himself? Shakespeare's artistic work, as it frequently is, is ambiguous. It's easy for us to interpret the witches psychologically as projections of Macbeth's own thoughts and desires. How else to understand the eerie similarity of his first words to the witches' earlier ones: "fair is foul, and foul is fair"? When he and Banquo enter, Macbeth's opening line is "So foul and fair a day I have not seen." (I, iii, 36) The day is certainly "foul" in terms of weather and "fair" in terms of the day's great victories. Does the similarity of their words indicate a secret psychic link between Macbeth and actual forces of evil? Does that place more of the responsibility on him or on unseen and malevolent forces?

It's remarkable that on hearing the witches' prophecy of his being king in the future he can envision *only* murder as the path to that goal. Blessed—or cursed—with the imaginative ability ascribed to all the water signs and vulnerable to the dark side of life as represented most especially by Scorpio, Macbeth immediately sees only a negative route to gaining the position of king. The temptation to do evil has begun.

Macbeth doesn't have to murder in order to get the throne. It's possible to gain a position higher than your current one through hard-won effort or by the decree of a sovereign. But attaining it unlawfully had serious consequences. The Elizabethans believed that seizing such a place illegitimately would not only rebound disastrously on the initiator but also threaten the integrity of all creation, from bottom to top.

The Consequences of Evil: In Nature, the Human Realm, and the State

The eruption of evil into the human world, instigated by Macbeth, affects not just him; it instigates disruption in nature, for all realms are subtly connected. Once Macbeth upsets the established hierarchy by killing the lawful king, nature itself synchronously reflects the upturned order. Lennox, who has accompanied Macduff to Macbeth's castle to wake Duncan, speaks of this:

> The night has been unruly. Where we lay
> Our chimneys were blown down, and, as
>   they say,
> Lamentings heard i' th' air; strange screams
>   of death,
> And prophesying with accents terrible
> Of dire combustion and confused events
> New-hatched to th' woeful time. The obscure
>   bird [the owl]
> Clamoured the livelong night. Some say the
>   earth
> Was feverous and did shake.
>
> (II, iii, 50-7)

Macbeth concurs in a line reeking with irony: "'Twas a rough night."

Disruption spreads further. Three more strange and unnatural events occur almost immediately after Duncan's death, revealed in the conversation between an old Man and Ross outside Macbeth's castle: darkness persists into the daytime; a falcon is killed by an owl; and Duncan's horses "Turned wild in nature, broke their stalls, flung out,/ Contending 'gainst obedience, as they would/ Make war with mankind." (II, iv, 16-18) That an owl, normally the prey of the bigger bird, attacks and kills a falcon is a reversal of the natural way of things.

As the play progresses, disasters and disruptions overwhelm the entire country. Macduff, fled to England to persuade Duncan's oldest son and heir to return and depose the tyrant Macbeth, reports to Malcolm that "Each new morn/ New widows howl, new orphans cry, new sorrows/ Strike heaven on the face, that it resounds/ As if it felt with Scotland . . ." (IV, iii, 4-7) After the invasion of the combined English and Scottish forces, the apparent uprooting of Birnam wood and its eerie movement up Dunsinane Hill seem strangely apt in light of the accumulating unnatural events in nature. Nature itself is turning against Macbeth.

The consequences of succumbing to evil are most potently and dramatically depicted through the degeneration of Macbeth himself. We see how precarious Macbeth's mental state is even before the murder of Duncan when he sees an imaginary dagger hanging in the air leading him toward Duncan's chamber. But the first significant sign of his broken bond with the grand design is that immediately after Duncan's death he cannot pronounce words of benediction. When some sleepers stir—and have psychically perceived that a murder has been committed—Macbeth is unable to join their instant invocation of divine protection.

> MACBETH: One cried 'God bless us!' and
> 'Amen' the other,
> As they had seen me with these hang-
> man's hands.
> List'ning their fear, I could not say
> 'Amen'
> When they did say 'God bless us.'
> LADY MACBETH: Consider it not so deeply.
> MACBETH: But wherefore could not I pro-
> nounce 'Amen'?
> I had most need of blessing, and 'Amen'
> Stuck in my throat.
>
> (II, ii, 24-31)

The worldview of Shakespeare's time is theocentric, that is, it originates with God or the Great Creative Power; in violating the ban against murder Macbeth has cut himself off from the Divine. Simultaneously he has cut himself off from himself, that is, from his own higher self: "To know my deed 'twere best not know myself./ Wake Duncan with thy knocking. I would thou couldst." (II, ii, 71-2)

Another indication that outward disorder is more and more internalized within Macbeth is that he's more and more unable to sleep. This too is a symptom of his greater disconnection with the established grand order, as well as the sign of a troubled personal conscience. Macbeth has brought this on himself, for immediately after the murder he hears a voice cry, "Sleep no more,/ Macbeth does murder sleep." (II, ii 33-4) He seems to have killed his own capacity to rest, be refreshed, and be restored to health through sleep. The inability to sleep spreads from Macbeth to others, for one of the Scottish lords, while revealing that Macduff is fled to England, hopes that "—with Him above/ To ratify the work—we may again/ Give to our tables meat, sleep to our nights . . ." (III, vi, 32-4)

A particular disruption of the night's rest is sleepwalking—and we see vividly the consequences of embarking on a course of evil in the inadvertent revelation of Lady Macbeth's haunted CONSCIENCE while she sleepwalks in the castle late in the play. Macbeth, too, has suffered "terrible dreams that shake [him] nightly." (III, ii, 20-1)

So Macbeth has no rest and no peace. A dominant psychological need for a Scorpio is SECURITY, which drives the Scorpio compulsion to have control (and therefore power) over yourself and your environment. For Macbeth, though, instead of achieving a comfortable situation once he has become king, he becomes more and more *in*secure. "To be thus is nothing/ But to be safely thus," he worries, now transferring his anxieties to Banquo. (III, i, 49-50) Lady Macbeth, his feminine Scorpio counterpart, also feels she's on shaky ground: "Naught's had, all's spent,/ Where our *desire* is got without content./ 'Tis safer to be that which we destroy/ Than by destruction dwell in doubtful joy." (III, ii, 6-9)

As he becomes less and less secure, Macbeth is more and more fearful. Of all the emotions that a Scorpio can be subject to, FEAR, the opposite of Martial courage (since every astrological symbol contains its opposite), dominates him. Macbeth's underlying fears—of not being manly enough, of being shamed by his wife, of his crimes being discovered, of Banquo as a living rebuke to his regicide, of being disliked and deposed by his people—more and more obsess him and increase his insecurity.

After he has instructed and sent the two murderers to kill Banquo and his son, a third murderer suddenly appears. The second murderer protests, "He needs not our *mistrust*, since he delivers/ Our offices and what we have to do/ To the direction just." (III, iii, 3-4) (Literary critics speculate that the third murderer may be Macbeth himself, so unsure about their capabilities as hired assassins that he lurks in the background to monitor their efforts.) When Fleance escapes, Macbeth laments, "But now I am cabined, cribbed, confined, bound in/ To *saucy doubts and fears*." (III, iv, 23-4) Suspicious of the loyalty of his subjects, he reveals that "There's not a one of them but in his house/ I keep a servant fee'd." (III, iv, 130-1)

This is a critical point in the play, for now Macbeth determines to take the initiative and seek the witches, being "bent to know/ By the worst means the worst." He reduces everything to his own ego's needs, committing himself to complete SELFISHNESS, the bane of Scorpios:

"For mine own good/ All causes shall give way." Now he consciously acknowledges that there's no turning back, for he is "in blood stepped in so far that, should I wade no more,/ Returning were as tedious as go o'er." (III, iv, 131-7)

The steady deterioration of Macbeth coincides with increasing disorder within the ranks of the nobles. The thanes, arriving at Macbeth's castle in Forres to celebrate his new honor, are urged by him to take their seats according to their status: "You know your own degrees; sit down." (III, iv, 1) But by the end of the scene, after Macbeth falls into a fit of passion and seems to lose his reason after seeing Banquo's ghost, Lady Macbeth rebukes him, saying "You have displaced the mirth, broke the good meeting/ With most admired *disorder*," and requests that the thanes "*Stand not upon the order of your going,*/ But go at once." (III, iv, 108-9, 118-9) In Shakespeare's worldview, all levels are connected: when one person admits evil into his being, all of nature, all of the human realms, the great cosmos itself becomes disordered and suffers as a result.

Another of the terrible consequences of embarking on what the Porter describes as "the primrose way to th' ever-lasting bonfire" (II, iii, 17-8) is progressive isolation. Unable to trust anyone (witness the third murderer) or to unburden himself even to Lady Macbeth, Macbeth is more and more removed from human connection. Previously when he writes to her after the battle, he addresses her as "my dearest partner of greatness" (I, v, 9-10); when he arrives at their castle ahead of Duncan and his retinue, he greets her as "My dearest love." (I, v, 56) They plan the death of Duncan as a couple, collaborating on the plan and its execution, working together both before and after. But Macbeth arranges for the death of Banquo without any contribution from her. In fact she knows nothing about it. And Macbeth doesn't want her to know anything in advance: "Be innocent of the knowledge, dearest chuck,/ Till thou applaud the deed." (III, ii, 46-7) This suggests that he's looking to gain points for masculinity by orchestrating something dastardly on his own.

The deep love Macbeth and Lady Macbeth shared in a close working relationship dissipates under the terrible pressure of their criminal acts. This is entirely in line with the propensity of Mars, in contrast to Venus, to separate rather than to bring together. Macbeth now keeps himself aloof from her. She plaintively asks, "Why do you keep alone,/ Of sorriest fancies your companions making . . . ?" (III, ii, 10-1) (Scorpios are notorious loners.)

After the banquet scene, when Macbeth basically loses it, we never see Macbeth and Lady Macbeth together again. She appears only once more, briefly, at the very end of the play in the sleepwalking scene. In her ramblings, witnessed by the gentlewoman and the doctor, she reveals that she's lost in an inner underworld. The doctor reports to Macbeth that she's not physically ill, but "is troubled with thick-coming fancies/ That keep her from her rest." (V, iii, 40-1) The next we hear of her is that she is dead by her own hand. Embarking on a career of crime has destroyed their relationship—and ended her life.

Macbeth is more and more removed, too, from his peers. His closest friend and co-captain in the battles is Banquo. After they both witness the witches' prognostications, Macbeth invites Banquo to talk with him, saying, "Think upon what hath chanced, and at more time,/ The interim having weighed it, let us speak/ Our free hearts each to other." (I, iii, 152-4) We don't know whether they do converse later, but it's notable that at this point Macbeth is reaching out to Banquo to help him process what they've seen. The night of the murder, when Banquo restlessly walks within Macbeth's castle and encounters a figure he cannot at first identify, he asks, "Who's there?" That person is Macbeth who responds, "A friend." (II, i, 9-10) Yet soon Macbeth plots to have him killed.

In the final scenes we see that Macbeth's subjects are alienated from him too. One of the invading lords, Angus, observes that "Those he commands move only in command,/ Nothing in love." (V, ii, 19-20) Eventually Macbeth also acknowledges that he has sacrificed the lasting comforts of advanced years for the precarious position of king:

> I have lived long enough. My way of life
> Is fall'n into the sear, the yellow leaf,
> And that which should accompany old age,
> As honour, love, obedience, *troops of friends*,
> I must not look to have, but in their stead

Curses, not loud but deep, mouth-honour,
    breath
Which the poor heart would fain deny and
    dare not.

(V, iii, 23-9)

As Macbeth accumulates more and more murders to his account, he sinks lower and lower in the hierarchy of being, until he is at the animal level: "They have tied me to a stake. I cannot fly,/ But bear-like I must fight the course." (V, vii, 1-2) "Bear-like", Macbeth knows that he's trapped. As the play progresses, darker and darker epithets are applied to him: he's a "tyrant" (III, vi, 25), then "black Macbeth" (IV, iii, 53), "a devil . . . damn'd in evils" (IV, iii, 57), and lastly, in final hand-to-hand combat, Macduff addresses him as a "hell-hound." (V, x, 3) In the long-awaited confrontation with the avenger "not of woman born", the tyrant is destroyed. He has progressively left the human kingdom, dropped to the animal level, then to the realm of hell, and finally, in ultimate isolation, into nothingness.

Scorpio: From Degeneration to Regeneration

While Scorpio symbolism embraces possible disintegration on the physical, emotional, or mental levels, it also carries the promise of transformation, a restoration not just of the original state but the creation of one that includes a wisdom born of enduring suffering or surviving ordeals. For this to happen, according to worldview of Shakespeare's time the hero-villain must inevitably die. The realm must be purged of evil; only the death of the scapegoat-hero will allow for a fresh start. In *Macbeth* the new regime will be inaugurated under the leadership of Duncan's previously named heir, Malcolm.

We might expect Malcolm to be a "good guy" because he is the son of a commendable ruler. His father had a generous spirit, praising Macbeth and the other conquering fighters with no signs of envy or resentment for their outstanding achievements. Duncan rewards Macbeth in particular with a new title and sends his wife a diamond. The fact that diamonds are the highest in the category of gems indicates Duncan's inner quality. Significantly, diamonds are under the rulership of Mars, perhaps because of their hardness and ability to cut into other substances while remaining whole—a positive manifestation of Mars. Some of Duncan's innate goodness, along with his mother's, has devolved onto Malcolm. Macduff praises their virtue in saying to Malcolm, "Thy royal father/ Was a most sainted king. The queen that bore thee,/ Oftener upon her knees than on her feet,/ Died every day she lived." (IV, iii, 109-12)

In important ways, though, Malcolm is a vastly better choice of ruler than his father. Duncan was good-hearted but naïve, an innocent too easily taken in by appearances. He knew this about himself, commenting on his mistaken assessment of the traitorous Cawdor that "There's no art/ To find the mind's construction in the face./ He was a gentleman in whom I built/ An absolute trust." (I, iv, 11-14) Since he immediately greets Macbeth as "worthiest cousin!", he's obviously being taken in again. He pays the price for his too-trusting nature with his life.

Malcolm, on the other hand, has the wit to realize that he and his brother are in danger immediately after his father's murder, sensing that "This murderous shaft that's shot/ Hath not yet lighted, and our safest way/ Is to avoid the aim." (II, iii, 137-9) So he escapes to England.

Later, after Macduff flees to England to urge him to invade Scotland and depose Macbeth, Malcolm carefully tests Macduff's sincerity. Suspecting Macduff's motives, since others have petitioned him to arm against Macbeth, Malcolm employs an stratagem, a very Scorpionic trick, designed to test Macduff's sincerity: he assures Macduff that he's so full of vices that Scotland would be better ruled by "black" Macbeth. In so doing he's pretending to be the opposite of what he truly is. This, of course, is precisely contrary to the Macbeths' Machiavellian scheme of masking their evil intentions with outward goodness. Malcolm covers his innate goodness with a pretense of evil.

Malcolm first specifies two of the Scorpio vices, LUST and GREED, as his particular flaws. The first he describes as an unquenchable sexual appetite: ". . . there's no bottom, none, /To my voluptuousness." (IV, iii, 61-2) The second he avows is "a staunchless avarice," which will result in a hunger for the nobles' lands, jewels and houses. (IV, iii, 79) The troubled Macduff counters by saying that these traits might be counterbalanced by other graces to offset the two. But Malcolm protests that he has none, not one of the " king-becoming graces,/ As justice, verity, temp'rance, stableness,/ Bounty, perseverance, mercy, lowliness,/ Devotion, patience, courage, fortitude . . . " (IV, iii, 92-5)

Pushed beyond patience, Macduff explodes: "Fit to govern?/ No, not to live." (IV, iii, 103-4) With Macduff about to depart in disgust, Malcolm accepts that he is genuinely what he presents himself to be and reveals the motivation for his trick: "Devilish Macbeth/ By many of these trains hath sought to win me/ Into his power, and *modest wisdom plucks me/ From over-credulous haste . . .*" (IV, iii, 118-21) Thus Malcolm exhibits both the "wisdom of the serpent" and the harmlessness of the dove in testing before trusting Macduff. He recants his former statements and paints a picture of himself almost too good to be true. (See IV, iii, 124-33)

Most especially, Malcolm mentions that he's a virgin. It's unusual in a Mars-oriented play for a male to admit chastity, commonly valued in women and not in men, but as we near the end of the play the feminine and the feminine virtues are on the rise. This is essential if peace (associated with Venus) is to come to Scotland. Symbolically, at the end Venus must overcome Mars. Malcolm's strength of will in mastering desire and honoring his values demonstrates a degree of self-control that results from the positive discipline of the Scorpio type.

Macbeth—and Evil—Destroyed

Once the hero chooses to obey evil impulses, the classical conventions of tragedy decree an inevitable and ignoble death. His nature is so corrupted that his destiny is inescapably either to self-destruct or to be destroyed by a rightful avenger. Lady Macbeth's suicide illustrates the former. She who willingly—even exultantly—invoked the dark powers, bidding them to fill her "from the crown to the toe top-full/ Of direst cruelty" and to "Stop up th' access and passage to remorse" (I, v, 45-7) by the end of the drama sleepwalks, rubs her hands together uselessly to remove not just the physical but the moral stain, and moans "Hell is murky!" (V, i, 31) Ironically, she's overcome with remorse. Finally she "as 'tis thought, by self and violent hands/ Took off her life . . . " (V, xi, 36-7) The dark powers have toyed with her just as they did with Macbeth; her request to feel no guilt or regret for her actions is denied. In this play, as in most of Shakespeare's tragedies, the maxim holds: "evil is self-destroyed."

While Macbeth does not technically commit suicide, he goes to certain death. Confronted by the elected avenger Macduff, who is determined to exact satisfaction for the murder of his family, and disheartened by Macduff's revelation that he is not "of woman born", Macbeth knows that he's doomed. He first refuses to fight, until Macduff taunts him with

> Then yield thee, coward,
> And live to be the show and gaze o' th' time.
> We'll have thee, as our rarer monsters are,
> Painted upon a pole, and underwrit
> 'Here may you see the tyrant.'
>
> (V, x, 23-7)

His masculinity stung again (Macduff also knows how to use shaming and humiliation!), Macbeth elects not to live as a bound and disgraced captive but to fight to the end. Now we see a flash of the heroic bravery that he exhibited at the very beginning; we remember the Macbeth who displayed the positive virtues of Mars and whom Duncan excitedly acclaimed as "valiant cousin, worthy gentleman!" (I, ii, 24) Macbeth's last words are

> I will not yield,
> To kiss the ground before young Malcolm's
>   feet,
> And to be baited with the rabble's curse.
> Though Birnam Wood be come to Dun-
>   sinane,
> And thou oppos'd, being of no woman born,
> Yet I will try the last. Before my body
> I throw my *warlike* shield. Lay on, Macduff,
> And damn'd be him that first cries, 'Hold,
>   enough!'
>
> (V, x, 27-34)

And they exit fighting.

This play is a meditation on the Scorpionic topic of evil. It explores the ways in which evil can enter the human world, ripen, mature, and ultimately disintegrate in a spectacular and devastating cataclysm. We see the whole trajectory, from beginning to end. Macbeth was an admirable hero at the start, initially the incarnation of positive Mars: a brave noble, one who courageously defends the kingdom and so compels our admiration in line with Duncan's praise. But he transforms from a defender of country and King to a destroyer of country and King. We watch the stages of his gradual descent into evil, as he becomes trapped in a miasmic hell, unable to get off the path he travels or to reverse direction. He engages our sympathies and compels our horrified fascination as no other "villain" in Shakespeare does, for he's uncomfortably accessible to us. We have accompanied him on his journey, from the moment when he is described as slicing open Macdonwald's body to the moment when he retreats offstage, still fighting.

At the end of the play we are left with ever-recurring questions that are embedded in the zodiacal sign of Scorpio. Is evil real? And if it is, how and to what extent does it affect the human realm? Is there an external and eternal malignant force responsible for human sin and corruption? Can we ascribe much of the blame for Macbeth's tragedy to the demonic "weird sisters"? Western religion and spiritual philosophy have suggested three possible answers: first, that Evil is an independent principle, opposed to and as real as Good; second, that it exists but is subordinate to Good, as depicted in the Bible's Book of Job, where Satan reports to God about his testing of the poor tormented Israelite; or lastly, that it's an illusion, a nothingness that only appears to have power.

Shakespeare in his play *Macbeth* doesn't provide a definitive answer. Though the witches appear first before anyone else in the drama, implying that there are pre-existing evil forces that can work on the human psyche, there's equal emphasis on Macbeth's own desires and drives and on the influence of another powerful human being, his wife. As we contemplate the parabolic trajectory of Macbeth's career, Shakespeare, so often ambiguous, allows us to weigh all the elements and make up our own minds.

Shakespeare and the Stars
The Hidden Astrological Keys to Understanding the World's Greatest Playwright

Priscilla Costello, M.A.

- A unique interpretation of six of Shakespeare's best-known plays in light of astrological symbolism
- Explains the deep influences of astrology in the spiritual and philosophical worldview of Shakespeare's time
- Shows how the archetypes of astrology are the models for Shakespeare's vivid characters and the rationale for his language and imagery
- Draws on fundamental ideas of Western philosophy, mythology, religion, and esoteric wisdom as well as modern psychology

The first half of this unique and groundbreaking work provides necessary background for understanding Shakespeare's plays by describing the synthesis of both classical and Christian ideas of his time.

The second half examines six of Shakespeare's best-loved plays in the light of astrological symbolism, mythology, and modern depth psychology.

Thoroughly researched and well-illustrated, this book is a clear and brilliant synthesis that challenges conventional literary criticism of Shakespeare's works. By grounding its analysis in verifiable historical information, modern readers will find that this book illuminates the plays from a fresh perspective that deepens and profoundly transforms their understanding of them.

Please visit *PriscillaCostello.com* and
ShakespeareandtheStars.com for more information

Literature, Astrology, Psychology
528 pp. • 6 x 9 Paperback•Illustrations • $29.95
ISBN: 978-0-89254-216-1 • Ebook: 978-0-89254-631-2

Shakespeare and the Stars
Playbill Editions
PRISCILLA COSTELLO, M.A.

These six small books are 64 pages each and printed in a convenient trim size. They can be taken to theater performances or studied before and after reading or seeing a play.

These books celebrate the 400th anniversary of Shakespeare's death and offer fresh and exciting insights into the ever-popular works of the world's greatest playwright. Each analysis specifically highlights Shakespeare's use of the archetypal language of astrological symbolism in both obvious and subtle ways. Such references would have been well known in Shakespeare's time, but their deeper significance is lost to modern-day playgoers and readers.

The most unique aspect of these books is the revelation that many of Shakespeare's plays are entirely keyed to a specific zodiacal sign and its associated (or ruling) planet. Shakespeare's audience would have immediately grasped their significance in revealing character, foreshadowing the plot, and establishing key themes for each play.

The Merchant of Venice
ISBN: 978-0-89254-175-1
Ebook: 978-0-89254-642-8

The Tempest
ISBN: 978-0-89254-178-2
Ebook 978-0-89254-644-2

King Lear
ISBN: 978-0-89254-176-8
Ebook: 978-0-89254-643-5

Romeo and Juliet
ISBN: 978-0-89254-182-9
Ebook 978-0-89254-649-7

A Midsummer Night's Dream
ISBN: 978-0-89254-181-2
Ebook: 978-0-89254-648-0

Macbeth
ISBN: 978-0-89254-177-5
Ebook 978-0-89254-646-6

Each book is $11.00 • Paperback • 64 pp. • 5 ½ x 8 ½

PRISCILLA COSTELLO, M.A., Dipl. CAAE, is an educator, writer, speaker, and counseling astrologer. An enthusiastic lover of Shakespeare's work, she taught English language and literature for over 30 years. As a professional astrologer, she has the unique ability to synthesize Shakespeare's literary and astrological themes. Her double prize-winning M.A. thesis focused on religious philosophy and Jungian psychology. Founder and Director of The New Alexandria, a center for religious, spiritual, and esoteric studies, she is the author of *The Weiser Concise Guide to Practical Astrology* (2008) and *Shakespeare and the Stars: The Hidden Astrological Keys to Understanding the World's Greatest Playwright* (2016).

Please visit *PriscillaCostello.com* and *ShakespeareandtheStars.com* for more information